SEASONS *of* LOVE

AN ANTHOLOGY *of* POEMS & PROSE

Selected by

JOHN GREENHALGH

BROMPTON PRESS

In Springtime when the leaves are young,
Clear dewdrops gleam like jewels, hung
On boughs the fair birds roost among.

When Summer comes with sweet unrest,
Birds weary of their mother's breast,
And look abroad and leave the nest.

In Autumn ere the waters freeze,
The swallows fly across the seas:
If we could fly away with these!

In Winter when the birds are gone,
The sun himself looks starved and wan,
And starved the snow he shines upon.

CHRISTINA ROSSETTI 1830–1894
Seasons

Four seasons fill the measure of the year;
There are four seasons in the mind of Man:
He has his lusty Spring, when fancy clear
Takes in all beauty with an easy span:

He has his Summer, when luxuriously
Spring's honey'd cud of youthful thought he loves
To ruminate, and by such dreaming high
Is nearest unto heaven: quiet coves

His soul hath in its Autumn, when his wings
He furleth close; contented so to look
On mists in idleness — to let fair things
Pass by unheeded as a threshold brook:

He has his Winter too of pale misfeature,
Or else he would forego his mortal nature

JOHN KEATS 1794–1821

SPRING

Nothing is so beautiful as Spring —
    When weeds, in wheels, shoot long and lovely and lush;
    Thrush's eggs look little low heavens, and thrush
Through the echoing timber does so rinse and wring
The ear, it strikes like lightnings to hear him sing;
    The glassy peartree leaves and blooms, they brush
    The descending blue; the blue is all in a rush
With richness; the racing lambs too have fair their fling.

What is all this juice and all this joy?
    A strain of the earth's sweet being in the beginning
In Eden garden. — Have, get, before it cloy,
    Before it cloud, Christ, lord, and sour with sinning,
Innocent mind and Mayday in girl and boy,
    Most, O maid's child, thy choice and worthy the winning.

GERARD MANLEY HOPKINS 1844–1889
Spring

Once more the heavenly power
    Makes all things new,
And domes the red-plowed hills
    With loving blue;
The blackbirds have their wills
    The throstles, too.

ALFRED TENNYSON 1809–1892
from *Early Spring*

Do you ask what the birds say? The Sparrow, the Dove,
The Linnet and Thrush say, 'I love and I love!'
In the winter they're silent — the wind is so strong;
What it says, I don't know, but it sings a loud song,
But green leaves, and blossoms, and sunny warm weather
And singing, and loving — all come back together.
But the Lark is so brimful of gladness and love,
The green fields below him, the blue sky above,
Then he sings, and he sings; and for ever sings he —
'I love my Love, and my Love loves me!'

SAMUEL TAYLOR COLERIDGE 1772–1834
Answer to a Child's Question

The Joyes of *Parents* are Secret;
And so are their Griefes, and Feares:
They cannot utter the one; Nor they
will not utter the other.

FRANCIS BACON 1561–1626
from *Of Parents and Children*

My babe so beautiful! it thrills my heart
With tender gladness, thus to look at thee,
And think that thou shalt learn far other lore
And in far other scenes! For I was reared
In the great city, pent 'mid cloisters dim,
And saw naught lovely but the sky and stars.
But thou, my babe! shalt wander like a breeze
By lakes and sandy shores, beneath the clouds,
Which image in their bulk both lakes and shores
And mountain crags…

Therefore all seasons shall be sweet to thee,
Whether the summer clothe the general earth
With greenness, or the redbreast sit and sing
Betwixt the tufts of snow on the bare branch
Of mossy apple-tree, while the nigh thatch
Smokes in the sun-thaw; whether the eve-drops fall
Heard only in the trances of the blast,
Or if the secret ministry of frost
Shall hang them up in silent icicles,
Quietly shining to the quiet moon.

SAMUEL TAYLOR COLERIDGE 1772−1834
from *Frost at Midnight*

Tightly-folded bud,
I have wished you something
None of the others would:
Not the usual stuff
About being beautiful,
Or running off a spring
Of innocence and love —
They will all wish you that,
And should it prove possible,
Well, you're a lucky girl.

But if it shouldn't, then
May you be ordinary;
Have, like other women,
An average of talents:
Not ugly, not good-looking,
Nothing uncustomary
To pull you off your balance,
That, unworkable itself,
Stops all the rest from working.
In fact, may you be dull —
If that is what a skilled,
Vigilant, flexible,
Unemphasised, enthralled
Catching of happiness is called.

PHILIP LARKIN 1922–1985
Born Yesterday (for Sally Amis)

The boy was barely five years old.
We sent him to the little school
And left him there to learn the names
Of flowers in jam jars on the sill
And learn to do as he was told.
He seemed quite happy there until
Three weeks afterwards, at night,
The darkness whimpered in his room.
I went upstairs, switched on his light,
And found him wide awake, distraught,
Sheets mangled and his eiderdown
Untidy carpet on the floor.
I said, 'Why can't you sleep? A pain?'
He snuffled, gave a little moan,
And then he spoke a single word:
'Jessica.' The sound was blurred.
'Jessica? What do you mean?'
'A girl at school called Jessica,
She hurts —' he touched himself between
The heart and stomach '— she has been
Aching here and I can see her.'
Nothing I had read or heard
Instructed me in what to do.
I covered him and stroked his head.
'The pain will go, in time,' I said.

VERNON SCANNELL 1922–
Growing Pain

I ne'er was struck before that hour
    With love so sudden and so sweet.
Her face it bloomed like a sweet flower
    And stole my heart away complete.
My face turned pale as deadly pale,
    My legs refused to walk away,
And when she looked 'what could I ail?'
    My life and all seemed turned to clay.

And then my blood rushed to my face
    And took my sight away.
The trees and bushes round the place
    Seemed midnight at noonday.
I could not see a single thing,
    Words from my eyes did start;
They spoke as chords do from the string
    And blood burnt round my heart.

Are flowers the winter's choice?
    Is love's bed always snow?
She seemed to hear my silent voice
    And love's appeal to know.
I never saw so sweet a face
    As that I stood before:
My heart has left its dwelling-place
    And can return no more.

JOHN CLARE 1793–1864
First Love

How did the party go in Portman Square?
I cannot tell you; Juliet was not there.
And how did Lady Gaster's party go?
Juliet was next me and I do not know.

HILAIRE BELLOC 1870–1953
Juliet

All the breath and the bloom of the year in
    the bag of one bee:
All the wonder and wealth of the mine in the
    heart of one gem:
In the core of one pearl all and the shade and
    the shine of the sea:
Breath and bloom, shade and shine, — wonder,
    wealth, and — how far above them —
        Truth, that's brighter than gem,
        Trust, that's purer than pearl —
Brightest truth, purest trust in the universe —
        All were for me in the kiss of one girl.

ROBERT BROWNING 1812–1889
Summum Bonum

When you're young
Love sometimes confuses
It clouds the brain
And blows the fuses
How often during those tender years
You just can't see the wood for the tears.

ROGER McGOUGH 1937–

Love without hope, as when the young bird-catcher
Swept off his tall hat to the Squire's own daughter,
So let the imprisoned larks escape and fly
Singing about her head, as she rode by.

ROBERT GRAVES 1895–1985

When I was one-and-twenty
   I heard a wise man say,
'Give crowns and pounds and guineas
   But not your heart away;
Give pearls away and rubies
   But keep your fancy free.'
But I was one-and-twenty,
   No use to talk to me.

When I was one-and-twenty
   I heard him say again,
'The heart out of the bosom
   Was never given in vain;
'Tis paid with sighs a plenty
   And sold for endless rue.'
And I am two-and-twenty,
   And oh, 'tis true, 'tis true.

A E HOUSMAN 1859–1936

Never seek to tell your love,
Love that never told can be;
For the gentler wind does move
Silently, invisibly.

I told my love, I told my love.
I told her all my heart;
Trembling, cold, in ghastly fears,
Ah! she doth depart.

Soon as she was gone from me,
A traveller came by,
Silently, invisibly:
He took her with a sigh.

WILLIAM BLAKE 1757−1827

Now welcome Summer with thy sunnë soft,
That hast this winter's weathers overshake,
And driven away the longë nightës black.

Saint Valentine, that art full high aloft.
Thus singen smallë fowlës for thy sake:
Now welcome Summer with thy sunnë soft,
That hast this winter's weathers overshake.

Well have they cause for to gladden oft,
Since each of them recovered hath his make.
Full blissful may they singë when they wake:
Now welcome Summer with thy sunnë soft,
That has this winter's weathers overshake,
And driven away the longë nightës black!

GEOFFREY CHAUCER 1340?–1400
from *The Parliament of Fowls*

Shall I compare thee to a summer's day?
Thou art more lovely and more temperate:
Rough winds do shake the darling buds of May,
And summer's lease hath all too short a date:
Sometimes too hot the eye of heaven shines,
And often is his gold complexion dimmed,
And every fair from fair sometimes declines,
By chance, or nature's changing course untrimm'd;
But thy eternal summer shall not fade,
Nor lose possession of that fair thou ow'st,
Nor shall death brag thou wander'st in his shade,
When in eternal lines to time thou grow'st;
So long as men can breathe, or eyes can see,
So long lives this, and this gives life to thee.

WILLIAM SHAKESPEARE 1564–1616

Suppose I say *summer*,
write the word "hummingbird,"
put it in an envelope,
take it down the hill
to the box. When you open
my letter you will recall
those days and how much,
just how much, I love you.

RAYMOND CARVER 1938–1988
Hummingbird (for Tess)

My sweet Girl,

Your letter gave me more delight, than any thing in
the world but yourself could do; indeed I am almost
astonished that any absent one should have that luxurious
power over my senses which I feel. Even when I am not
thinking of you I receive your influence and a tenderer
nature steeling upon me. All my thoughts, my unhappiest
days and nights have I find not at all cured me of my love
of Beauty, but made it so intense that I am miserable that
you are not with me: or rather breathe in that dull sort of
patience that cannot be called Life. I never knew before,
what such a love as you have made me feel, was; I did not
believe in it; my fancy was affraid of it, lest it should burn
me up... I love you the more in that I believe you have
liked me for my own sake and for nothing else — I have
met with women whom I really think would like to be
married to a Poem and to be given away by a Novel...

Ever yours my love!

JOHN KEATS 1795—1821
To Fanny Brawne, 8 July 1819

My beloved spake, and said unto me,
Rise up, my love, my fair one, and come away.
For lo, the winter is past, the rain is over and gone;
The flowers appear on the earth;
the time of singing of birds is come,
and voice of the turtle is heard in our land;
The fig tree putteth forth her green figs, and the vines
with the tender grapes give a good smell.
Arise my love, my fair one, and come away.
O my dove, that art in the clefts of the rock, in the secret
places of the stairs, let me see thy countenance,
let me hear thy voice; for sweet is thy voice, and
thy countenance is comely.
Take us the foxes, the little foxes, that spoil the vines:
for our vines have tender grapes.
My beloved is mine, and I am his:
he feedeth among the lilies.

The Song of Solomon, 2:9–14

My true love hath my heart and I have his,
    By just exchange one for another given;
I hold his dear, and mine he cannot miss,
    There never was a better bargain driven.
        My true love hath my heart and I have his.

His heart in me keeps him and me in one,
    My heart in him his thoughts and senses guides;
He loves my heart, for once it was his own,
    I cherish his, because in me it bides.
        My true love hath my heart and I have his.

PHILIP SIDNEY 1554–1586

My heart is like a singing bird
    Whose nest is in a watered shoot;
My heart is like an apple-tree
    Whose boughs are bent with thickset fruit;
My heart is like a rainbow shell
    That paddles in a halcyon sea;
My heart is gladder than all these
    Because my love is come to me.

Raise me a dais of silk and down;
    Hang it with vair and purple dyes;
Carve it with doves, and pomegranates;
    And peacocks with a hundred eyes;
Work it in gold and silver grapes,
    In leaves, and silver fleurs-de-lys;
Because the birthday of my life
    Is come, my love is come to me.

CHRISTINA ROSSETTI 1830–1894
A Birthday

She wore a new 'terra-cotta' dress,
And we stayed, because of the pelting storm,
Within the hansom's dry recess,
Though the horse had stopped; yea, motionless
    We sat on, snug and warm.

Then the downpour ceased, to my sharp sad pain
And the glass that had screened our forms before
Flew up, and out she sprang to her door:
I should have kissed her if the rain
    Had lasted a minute more.

THOMAS HARDY 1840–1928
A Thunderstorm in Town (A Remembrance: 1893)

Country lovers play at love
In a scene all laid for loving…
Long dewy lanes invite the feet
And all the silver dust is sweet
With unimaginable roses…

…London lovers lack the aid
Of such poetic properties:
In uninspiring streets are played
Their love-scenes and their ecstasies.
They are not coached by moon or star
Or prompted by the nightingale;
On Shepherd's Bush no roses are;
There lies no dew in Maida Vale.
London lovers see instead
Electric sky-signs overhead,
Jarring upon romantic mood
With eulogies of patent food.
For them no peace when twilight falls,
Only the noise of busy places,
The drabness of a thousand walls,
The staring of a thousand faces.
Yet London man to London maid
Makes his undaunted serenade:
Enraptured and oblivious
He woos her — on a motor bus…

JAN STRUTHER 1901–1953
from *London Lovers*

She is living in Paradise Walk,
With the dirt and the noise of the street;
And heaven flies up, if she talk,
With Paradise down at her feet.

She laughs through a summer of curls;
She moves in a garden of grace;
Her glance is a treasure of pearls,
How saved from the deeps of her face!

And the magical reach of her thigh
Is the measure, with which God began
To build up the peace of the sky,
And fashion the pleasures of man.

With Paradise down at her feet,
While heaven flies up if she talk;
With the dirt and the noise of the street,
She is living in Paradise Walk.

HERBERT HORNE 1864–1916
Paradise Walk

With love so like fire they dared not
Let it out into strawy small talk;
With love so like flood they dared not
Let out a trickle lest the whole crack,

These two sat speechlessly:
Pale cool tea in tea-cups chaperoned
Stillness, silence, the eyes
Where fire and flood strained.

TED HUGHES 1930—
Parlour-piece

The grey sea and long black land,
And the yellow half-moon large and low;
And the startled little waves that leap
In fiery ringlets from their sleep,
As I gain the cove with the pushing prow,
And quench its speed i' the slushy sand.

Then a mile of warm sea-scented beach;
Three fields to cross till a farm appears;
A tap at the pane, the quick sharp scratch
And blue spurt of a lighted match,
And a voice less loud, thro' its joys and fears,
Than the two hearts beating each to each.

ROBERT BROWNING 1812−1889
Meeting at Night

Are you forgotten? Yes, I think you are,
forgotten with most other lovely things,
since but a stifled echo, faint and far,
is all distracted recollection brings.
For busy nothings have obsessed my days,
crowding the private places of my mind,
and every eager, starving sense decays
in seeking vainly where it may not find.
But when the tedious, empty clamour dies,
and Sleep, your pity-laden messenger,
stoops with her lips upon my closing eyes,
and Night's dark players make their entrance where
the shadowy stage of dreams is dimly set,
then I remember — how should I forget?

RICHARD ELWES 1901–1968

In darkness the loud sea makes moan,
And earth is shaken, and all evils creep
About her ways. Oh, now to know you sleep!
Out of the whirling blinding moil, alone,
Out of the slow grim fight,
One thought to wing — to you, asleep,
In some cool room that's open to the night,
Lying half-forward, breathing quietly,
One white hand on the white
Unrumpled sheet, and the ever-moving hair
Quiet and still at length!…

RUPERT BROOKE 1887–1915
from *The Charm*

Love is a sickness full of woes,
All remedies refusing;
A plant that with most cutting grows,
Most barren with best using.
           Why so?
More we enjoy it, more it dies;
If not enjoyed, it sighing cries,
           Hey ho.

Love is a torment of the mind,
A tempest everlasting;
And Jove hath made it of a kind,
Not well, nor full nor fasting.
           Why so?
More we enjoy it, more it dies;
If not enjoyed, it sighing cries,
           Hey ho.

SAMUEL DANIEL 1562–1619

Love, we must part now: do not let it be
Calamitous and bitter. In the past
There has been too much moonlight and self-pity:
Let us have done with it: for now at last
Never has sun more boldly paced the sky,
Never were hearts more eager to be free,
To kick down worlds, lash forests; you and I
No longer hold them; we are husks, that see
The grain going forward to a different use.

There is regret. Always, there is regret.
But it is better that our lives unloose,
As two tall ships, wind-mastered, wet with light,
Break from an estuary with their courses set,
And waving part, and waving drop from sight.

PHILIP LARKIN 1922−1985

AUTUMN

Season of mists and mellow fruitfulness,
    Close bosom-friend of the maturing sun;
Conspiring with him how to load and bless
    With fruit the vines that round the thatch-eaves run;
To bend with apples the moss's cottage-trees,
    And fill all fruit with ripeness to the core;
        To swell the gourd, and plump the hazel shells
With a sweet kernel; to set budding more,
    And still more, later flowers for the bees,
    Until they think warm days will never cease,
        For Summer has o'erbrimm'd their clammy cells...

JOHN KEATS 1795–1821
from *Ode to Autumn*

The long-lighted days begin to shrink,
And flowers are thin in mead, among
The late-shooting grass, that shines along
Brook upon brook, and brink by brink.

The wheat that was lately rustling thick,
Is now up in mows that still are new;
All yellow before the sky of blue,
Tip after tip, and rick by rick.

No starlings arise in flock on wing;
The cuckoo has still'd his woodland sound;
The swallow not longer wheels around,
Dip after dip, and swing by swing.

While shooters are roving round the knoll
By wind-driven leaves on quiv'ring grass;
O down where the sky-blue waters pass,
Fall after fall, and shoal by shoal;

Their brown-dappled pointers nimbly trot
By russet-boughed trees, while gun-smoke grey
Dissolves in the air of sunny day,
Reef upon reef, at shot by shot.

While now I can walk a dusty mile,
I'll take me a day, while days are clear,
To find a few friends that still are dear,
Face upon face, and smile upon smile,

WILLIAM BARNES 1801–1886
Autumn

Whene'er I see soft hazel eyes
    And nut-brown curls,
I think of those bright days I spent
    Among the Limerick girls;
When up though Cratla woods I went,
    Nutting with thee;
And we plucked the glossy clustering fruit
    From many a bending tree.

Beneath the hazel boughs we sat,
    Thou, love, and I,
And the gather'd nuts lay in thy lap,
    Beneath thy downcast eye:
But little we thought of the store we'd won,
    I, love, or thou;
For our hearts were full, and we dare not own
    The love that's spoken now.

Oh, there's wars for willing hearts in Spain,
    And high Germanie!
And I'll come back, ere long, again,
    With knightly fame and fee:
And I'll come back, if I ever come back,
    Faithful to thee,
That sat with thy white lap full of nuts
    Beneath the hazel tree.

SAMUEL FERGUSON 1810–1886
The Lapful of Nuts

Stella this day is thirty-four,
(We shan't dispute a year or more:)
However, Stella, be not troubled,
Though thy size and years are doubled
Since first I saw thee at sixteen,
The brightest virgin on the green;
So little is thy form declined;
Made up so largely in thy mind.

O, would it please the gods to split
Thy beauty, size, and years and wit!
No age could furnish out a pair
Of nymphs so graceful, wise and fair;
With half the lustre of your eyes,
With half your wit, your years, and size.
And then, before it grew too late,
How should I beg of gentle fate,
(That either nymph might have her swain,)
To split my worship too in twain.

JONATHAN SWIFT 1667–1745
Stella's Birth-day

How do I love thee? Let me count the ways.
    I love thee to the depth and breadth and height
    My soul can reach, when feeling out of sight
For the ends of Being and ideal Grace.
I love thee to the level of every day's
    Most quiet need, by sun and candlelight.
    I love thee freely, as men strive for Right;
I love thee purely, as they turn from Praise.
I love thee with the passion put to use
    In my old griefs, and with my childhood's faith.
I love thee with a love I seemed to lose
    With my lost saints — I love thee with the breath,
Smiles, tears, of all my life! — and, if God choose,
    I shall but love thee better after death.

ELIZABETH BARRETT BROWNING 1806–1861

I was so chill, and overworn, and sad,
To be a lady was the only joy I had.
I walked the street as silent as a mouse,
Buying fine clothes, and fittings for the house.

But since I saw my love
I wear a simple dress,
And happily I move
Forgetting weariness.

ANNA WICKHAM 1883—1947
Song

O wert thou in the cauld blast,
    On yonder lea, on yonder lea,
My plaidie to the angry airt,
    I'd shelter thee, I'd shelter thee.
Or did misfortune's bitter storms
    Around thee blaw, around thee blaw,
Thy bield should be my bosom,
    To share it a', to share it a'.

Or were I in the wildest waste,
    Sae black and bare, sae black and bare,
The desert were a Paradise,
    If thou wert there, if thou wert there.
Or were I monarch o' the globe,
    Wi' thee to reign, wi' thee to reign,
The brightest jewel in my crown
    Wad be my queen, wad be my queen.

ROBERT BURNS 1759–1796

i carry your heart with me(i carry it in
my heart)i am never without it(anywhere
i go you go,my dear;and whatever is done
by only me is your doing,my darling)
                                        i fear
no fate(for you are my fate,my sweet)i want
no world(for beautiful you are in my world,my true)
and it's you are whatever a moon has always meant
and whatever a sun will always sing is you

here is the deepest secret nobody knows
(here is the root of the root and the bud of the bud
and the sky of the sky of a tree called life;which grows
higher than soul can hope or mind can hide)
and this is the wonder that's keeping the stars apart

i carry your heart(i carry it in my heart)

E E CUMMINGS 1894–1962

Alas! is even love too weak
To unlock the heart, and let it speak?
Are even lovers powerless to reveal
To one another what indeed they feel?
I knew the mass of men concealed
Their thoughts, for fear that if revealed
They would by other men be met
With blank indifference, or with blame reproved;
I knew they lived and moved
Tricked in disguises, alien to the rest
Of men, and alien to themselves — and yet
The same heart beats in every human breast!...

Only — but this is rare —
When a belovèd hand is laid in ours,
When, jaded with the rush and glare
Of the interminable hours,
Our eyes can in another's eyes read clear,
When our world-deafened ear
Is by the tones of a loved voice caressed —
A bolt is shot back somewhere in our breast,
And a lost pulse of feeling stirs again.
The eye sinks inward, and the heart lies plain,
And what we mean, we say, and what we would, we know.
A man becomes aware of his life's flow,
And hears its winding murmur; and he sees
The meadows where it glides, the sun, the breeze...

MATTHEW ARNOLD 1822–1888
from *The Buried Life*

We are all liars, because
the truth of yesterday becomes a lie tomorrow,
whereas letters are fixed,
and we live by the letter of truth.
The love I feel for my friend, this year,
is different from the love I felt last year.
If it were not so, it would be a lie.
Yet we reiterate love! love! love!
as if it were a coin with a fixed value
instead of a flower that dies, and opens a different bud.

D H LAWRENCE 1885–1935
Lies About Love

A pity beyond all telling
Is hid in the heart of love:
The folk who are buying and selling,
The clouds on their journey above,
The cold wet winds ever blowing,
And the shadowy hazel grove
Where mouse-grey waters are flowing,
Threaten the head that I love.

WB YEATS 1865–1939
The Pity of Love

My little Son, who looked from thoughtful eyes
And moved and spoke in quiet grown-up wise,
Having my law the seventh time disobeyed,
I struck him, and dismissed
With hard words and unkissed…

Then, fearing lest his grief should hinder sleep,
I visited his bed,
But found him slumbering deep,
With darkened eyelids, and their lashes yet
From his late sobbing wet.

And I, with moan,
Kissing away his tears, left others of my own;
He had put, within his reach,
A box of counters and a red-veined stone,
A piece of glass abraded by the beach,
And six or seven shells,
A bottle with bluebells,
And two French copper coins, ranged there
    with careful art,
To comfort his sad heart.
So when that night I prayed
To God, I wept, and said:
'Ah, when at last we lie with tranced breath,
Not vexing Thee in death,
And Thou rememberest of what toys
We made our joys,
How weakly understood
Thy great commanded good,
Then, fatherly not less
Than I whom Thou has moulded from the clay,
Thou'lt leave Thy wrath and say,
"I will be sorry for their childishness."'

COVENTRY PATMORE 1823–1896
The Toys

WINTER

Frost
sharpens
church spires
to a fine point,
pares down trees
to their
deep-set bones

MOIRA ANDREW

Here is not colour, here but form and structure,
The bones of trees, the magpie bark of birches…

Apse of trees and tracery of network,
Fields of snow and tranquil trees in snow…

VITA SACKVILLE-WEST 1892–1962
from *The Land*

He comes on chosen evenings,
My blackbird beautiful, and sings
Over the gardens of the town
Just at the hour the sun goes down.
His flight across the chimneys thick,
By some divine arithmetic,
Comes to his customary stack,
And couches there his plumage black,
And there he lifts his yellow bill
Kindled against the sunset, till
These suburbs are like Dymock woods
Where music has her solitudes,
And while he mocks the winter's wrong
Rapt on his pinnacle of song,
Figured above our garden plots
These are celestial chimney-pots.

JOHN DRINKWATER 1882–1937
Blackbird

I, singularly moved
To love the lovely that are not beloved,
Of all the seasons, most
Love Winter, and to trace
The sense of the Trophonian pallor on her face.
It is not death, but plenitude of peace;
And the dim cloud that does the world enfold
Hath less the characters of dark and cold
Than warmth and light asleep,
And correspondent breathing seems to keep
With the infant harvest, breathing soft below
Its eider coverlet of snow...

COVENTRY PATMORE 1823–1896
from *Winter*

Coming up Buchanan Street, quickly, on a sharp
    winter evening
a young man and two girls, under the Christmas lights —
The young man carries a new guitar in his arms,
the girl on the inside carries a very young baby,
and the girl on the outside carries a chihuahua.
And all three of them are laughing, their breath rises
in a cloud of happiness, and as they pass

the boy says, 'Wait till he sees this but!'
The chihuahua has a tiny Royal Stewart tartan coat
    like a teapot-holder,
the baby in its white shawl all bright eyes and mouth
    like favours in a fresh sweet cake,
the guitar swells out under its milky plastic cover,
    tied at the neck with silver tinsel tape and
    a brisk sprig of misteltoe.
Orphean sprig! Melting baby! Warm chihuahua!
The vale of tears is powerless before you.
Whether Christ is born, or is not born, you
put paid to fate, it abdicates
                    under the Christmas lights.

Monsters of the year
go blank, are scattered back,
can't bear this march of three.

— And the three have passed, vanished in the crowd
(yet not vanished, for in their arms they wind
the life of men and beasts, and music,
laughter ringing them round like a guard)
at the end of this winter's day.

EDWIN MORGAN 1920–
Trio

Softly, in the dusk, a woman is singing to me;
Taking me back down the vista of years, till I see
A child sitting under the piano, in the boom of the
    tingling strings
And pressing the small poised feet of a mother who
    smiles as she sings.

In spite of myself, the insidious mastery of song
Betrays me back, till the heart of me weeps to belong
To the old Sunday evenings at home, with winter outside
And hymns in the cosy parlour, the tinkling piano
    our guide.

So now it is vain for the singer to burst into clamour
With the great black piano appassionato. The glamour
Of childish days is upon me, my manhood is cast
Down in the flood of remembrance, I weep like a child
    for the past.

D H LAWRENCE 1885–1935
Piano

Making the marmalade this year, I carve
Some peel to form the initial of your name.

Perhaps you'll come across it when I'm gone,
For even in mourning mornings will go on.

So such surprise as ancient love contrives
Will change to the kind of shock that stunned our prime.

ROY FULLER 1912–1991
Preserving

On a mid-December day,
frying sausages
for myself, I abruptly
felt under my fingers
thirty years younger the rim
of a steering-wheel,
on my cheek the parching wind
of an August noon,
as passenger beside me
You as then you were.

Slap across a veg-growing
alluvial plain
we raced in clouds of white dust,
and geese fled screaming
as we missed them by inches,
making a bee-line
for mountains gradually
enlarging eastward,
joyfully certain nightfall
would occasion joy.

It did. In a flagged kitchen
we were served broiled trout
and a rank cheese: for a while
we talked by the fire,
then, carrying candles, climbed
steep stairs. Love was made
then and there: so halcyoned,

soon we fell asleep
to the sound of a river
swabbling through a gorge.

Since then, other enchantments
have blazed and faded,
enemies changed their address,
and War made ugly
an uncountable number
of unknown neighbors,
precious as us to themselves:
but round your image
there is no fog, and the Earth
can still astonish.

Of what, then, should I complain,
pottering about
a neat suburban kitchen?
Solitude? Rubbish!
It's social enough with real
faces and landscapes
for whose friendly countenance
I at least can learn
to live with obesity
and a little fame.

W H AUDEN 1907–1973
Since

Once I was part of the music I heard
    On the boughs or sweet between earth and sky,
    For joy of the beating of wings on high
My heart shot into the breast of the bird.

I hear it now and I see it fly,
    And a life in wrinkles again is stirred;
    My heart shoots into the breast of the bird
As it will for sheer joy till the last long sigh.

GEORGE MEREDITH 1828–1909
This Fragile Frame

The ring, so worn as you behold,
So thin, so pale, is yet of gold.
The passion such it was to prove:
Worn with life's care, love yet was love.

GEORGE CRABBE 1754–1832

He first deceased; she for a little tried
To live without him, liked it not, and died.

HENRY WOTTON 1568–1639
Upon the Death of Sir Albert Morton's Wife

Dull sublunary lovers' love
    (Whose soule is sense) cannot admit
Absence, because it doth remove
    Those things that elemented it.

But we by a love, so much refin'd,
    That our selves know not what it is,
Inter-assured of the mind,
    Care lesse, eyes, lips, and hands to misse.

Our two soules therefore, which are one,
    Though I must goe, endure not yet
A breach, but an expansion,
    Like gold to ayery thinnesse beate…

JOHN DONNE 1572–1631
from *A Valediction, Forbidding Mourning*

'I often say to myself: suppose one
could start one's life over again, but
this time with full knowledge?
Suppose one could live one's life as
one writes a school composition,
once in rough draft, and then live it
again in fair copy?…'

ANTON CHEKHOV 1860–1909
Captain Vershinin in *The Three Sisters*

And did you get what
you wanted from this life, even so?
I did.
And what did you want?
To call myself beloved, to feel myself
beloved on the earth.

RAYMOND CARVER 1938–1988
Late Fragment

ACKNOWLEDGEMENTS

Moira Andrew, 52: from *This Poem Doesn't Rhyme* (1990) published by Viking Books, by permission of the author.

W H Auden, 58: from *Collected Poems* (1976), by permission of Faber and Faber Limited.

Hilaire Belloc, 15: from *Sonnets and Verses* (1954), reprinted by permission of Peters, Fraser & Dunlop Group Limited.

Raymond Carver, 22 and 58: 'Hummingbird' and 'Late Fragment' from *A New Path to the Waterfall*, first published by Atlantic Monthly Press 1989. First published in Great Britain by Collins Harvill 1989. Copyright © Tess Gallagher. Reproduced by permission of The Harvill Press.

E.E. Cummings, 45: reprinted from *Complete Poems 1904–1962*, by E.E.Cummings, edited by George J. Firmage, by permission of W.W. Norton & Company Ltd. Copyright © 1952, 1980, 1991 by the Trustees for the E.E. Cummings Trust.

John Drinkwater, 53: from *Collected Poems* (1923). Reproduced by permission of the Estate of John Drinkwater and Samuel French Limited.

Richard Elwes, 32: from *First Poems* (1940) published Hodder and Stoughton, reprinted by permission of David Higham Associates.

Roy Fuller, 57: from *Consolations* (1987) published by Secker and Warburg, reprinted by permission of Reed Consumer Books.

Robert Graves, 13: from *Complete Poems* (1995), reprinted by Carcanet Press Limited.

Thomas Hardy, 27: from *Complete Poems of Thomas Hardy* (1976), by permission of Papermac.

A E Housman, 16: from *A Shropshire Lad*, by permission of The Society of Authors as the literary representative of the Estate of A E Housman.

Ted Hughes, 30: from *The Hawk in the Rain*, by permission of Faber and Faber Limited.

Philip Larkin, 10 and 35: from *Collected Poems*, by permission of Faber and Faber Limited and The Marvell Press, England & Australia.

D H Lawrence, 47 and 56: from *Complete Poems* (1972) reprinted by permission of Laurence Pollinger Limited and the Estate of Frieda Lawrence Ravagli.

Roger McGough, 12: from *Sky in the Pie*, (1983) reprinted by permission of Peters, Fraser & Dunlop Group Limited.

Edwin Morgan, 24: from *Collected Poems*, by permission of Carcanet Press Limited.

Vita Sackville-West, 52: from *The Land*, © 1927 Vita Sackville-West, reproduced by permission of Curtis Brown, London.

Vernon Scannell, 11: from *Collected Poems (1950–1993)*, by permission of Robson Books.

Jan Struther, 28: from 'London Lovers' copyright Jan Struther, reproduced by permission of Curtis Brown Group Limited, London.

Anna Wickham, 43: from *Selected Poems* (1971). Copyright © The Estate of the Author, by permission of Random House UK Limited.

W B Yeats, 48: from *Collected Poems* by permission of AP Watt Limited on behalf of Michael Yeats.

First published in Great Britain 1997 by Brompton Press, 100 Brompton Road, London SW3 1ER
Copyright © Brompton Press 1997
ISBN 1 900055 06 6
British Library Cataloguing in Publication Data. Data available.
Design: johnson banks
Photography: Carol Sharp
Production: Deer Park Productions
Printed in England by Butler & Tanner Limited